THE CRAWrISH

How to: Techniques, Baits, Traps and Great Recipes

BY

ANTHONY NELSON

TABLE OF CONTENTS

ABOUT THE AUTHOR

Anthony Nelson is an entrepreneur, author, business owner and avid outdoorsmen. He has helped many people realize their dream of business ownership. Together with his wife Jennifer, they founded and are owners of SHS Franchising. SHS Franchising is the parent company of Spectrum Home Services. Spectrum Home Services is a very successful home services business that was start in 2000 by both Anthony and Jenny. It was so successful that they chose to begin franchising the concept in 2004.

Anthony Nelson is a graduate of California State University Long Beach with a degree in Political Science. He Lives in Salt Lake City with his wife Jennifer and his two children Jacob and AnnMarie.

This book is designed to help you enjoy the sport of fishing for crawfish. Anthony is a firm believer that the more time you spend in the outdoors with your children the better citizens and members of society they will become. Fishing for Crawfish is a blast for adults and youth alike and is a great way to bring people together for a good time outdoors.

INTRODUCTION

The latest culinary craze to sweep the country has been centered on a little fresh water crustacean – the crawfish. These aquatic delicacies inhabit lakes, ponds and rivers and are probably in water habitats close to your hometown.

Crawfish look like little Maine lobsters and when cooked properly are as tasty as their ocean cousins. The best thing about crawfish is that they are fun to catch with family and friends and make a delicious feast.

In Sweden, they celebrate the crawfish every August. It is part of their long tradition and culture. The whole country takes a summer evening to boil and feast on crawfish. The evening also includes good drink, laughter and a celebration of summer. Just think how much better the world would be if every country spent one night in celebration.

My family now has a new tradition. Every year we go deer hunting up in the Wasatch National Forest near Strawberry Reservoir. The beautiful colors of the aspen and oaks are splashed against the beautiful dark green background of majestic pines and spruce trees.

Located near our campsite is Strawberry Reservoir. Strawberry is a prolific Cutthroat trout and crawfish fishery. Over the years, we have come to enjoy the catching of crawfish as much as hunting for deer. Many afternoons, you will find our camp empty as everyone is down at the lake catching crawfish for the many different types of crawfish recipes we prepare over the campfire.

I hope that after you read this short book on crawfish, it will inspire you to get outdoors with your family and friends and spend time enjoying what nature has provided us. Catch a bucket load of crawfish and spend an evening celebrating summer while feasting on your catch.

Fishing for crawfish will bring you closer to the ones you love and will make memories that will last a lifetime. All you need is a piece of twine, a chicken leg and a willingness to try something new. You never know, you might start a new family tradition!

Everyone is at the lake catching crawfish!

CHAPTER 1

A LITTLE INFORMATION ON THE CRAWFISH

Crawfish – also called crayfish, or crawdads are freshwater crustaceans resembling small lobsters, to which they are related. Crawfish are found in bodies of water that do not freeze to the bottom. They are mostly found in brooks and streams where there is fresh water running, and which have shelter against predators.

Most crawfish cannot tolerate polluted water, although some species such as the Red Swamp Crawfish are hardier and can be found in less than pristine water conditions.

Crawfish feed on living and dead animals and plants. Some kinds of crawfish are known locally as lobsters, crawdads, or mudbugs. In the Eastern United States, "crayfish" is more common in the north, while "crawdad" is heard more in central and southwestern regions, and "crawfish" further south.

Over 350 of the world's approximately 500 species of crawfish live in the streams and lakes of the United States. The majority of crawfish species occur east of the Rocky Mountains and in the Southeastern states.

About 65 of the 350 crawfish species in North America are endangered; nearly half of the native crawfish species have been estimated as needing protection. Habitat loss is the leading cause of population declines or extinction for aquatic animals; the second leading cause is the introduction of nonnative organisms.

Nonnative crawfish are a major threat to aquatic biodiversity. They cause the decline of native crawfish by spreading crawfish diseases, and they prey upon eggs, young fish, amphibians and native crawfish, as well as eliminating native water plants and habitats. On average, crawfish grow to 6.9 inches in length, but some grow larger.

North America

The greatest diversity of crawfish species is found in southeastern North America, with over 330 species. Many crawfish are also found in lowland areas where water is abundant.

Crawfish were introduced purposely into reservoirs in many states and other bodies of water decades ago, primarily as a food source for sport fish. They have since dispersed beyond those original sites. Currently all states have crawfish populations.

Crawfish as Food

Crawfish are eaten worldwide. Just like their larger cousin the lobster, only a small portion of the crawfish is edible. In most recipes only the tail portion is served.

At crawfish boils or other meals where the entire body of the crawfish is served you can crack the claws and eat what little bit of meat might be in the claw. Also, the juices from the head can be sucked out.

Bait

Crawfish are commonly sold and used as bait, either live or with only the tail meat, and are good at attracting Catfish, Bass, Pike and Muskie. Sometimes the claws are removed so that the crawfish don't stop fish from biting the hook. Crawfish easily fall off the hook, so casting should be performed slowly and carefully.

The result of using crawfish as bait has led to various ecological problems at times. The use of crawfish as bait has been cited as one of the ways non-native species have spread to different waterways. Many crawfish that are used for bait actually survive the hook and populate previously unpopulated crawfish waters. In some states, it is illegal to transport live crawfish from the water you caught them in. These laws are on the books to prevent the introduction of invasive crawfish into other waters. Crawfish are voracious eaters and invasive species of crawfish quickly out forage and out reproduce the natural populations of crawfish.

Pets- Crawfish are kept as pets in freshwater aquariums and backyard ponds. Crawfish kept as pets are usually not compatible with goldfish or other small tropical fish species.

Habitat and Diet - Crawfish prefer clean water. Habitat can be found in rivers, streams, lakes, ponds, irrigation ditches and swamps.

Crawfish activity is focused on the quest for food. If food sources are abundant, a crawfish will only have to forage a limited amount of time. When food is scarce, though, crawfish will spend a considerable amount of time foraging. Crawfish consume both plants and animals. Aquatic plants, molluscs, insect larvae, mature insects, tadpoles, amphibian eggs, and small fish are common foods. Crawfish tend to forage for food at night. Night is also the best time to catch crawfish since this is their primary feeding time.

Moulting - Just like its more famous cousin the lobster, crawfish need to moult to grow. When a crawfish moults it is very vulnerable to becoming a predator's lunch. When they moult they will stay out of sight in their holes for up to 5 days. Crawfish can moult anywhere from 3 times to 10 times a year depending on their age.

Common Cray Fish in North America-

The Calico Crawfish- This crawfish species is known as the Northern Crawfish and is found throughout Canada and the United States.

The Virilis Crawfish- A common North American crawfish species.

The Rusty Crawfish- This crawfish is rapidly expanding its range in North America and is displacing native crawfish species.

The Pilose Crawfish- This crawfish is wide ranging in the Pacific Northwest, Rocky Mountains and California.

The Red Swamp Crawfish- Red Crawfish are the species of crawfish that provides the bulk of crawfish eaten in restaurants and at crawfish boils.

The White River Crawfish- A common crawfish used in the commercial production of crawfish.

The Signal Crawfish- This species is native to North America but was introduced into Europe. It has caused serious declines in native European Crawfish stocks due to its tendency to carry Crawfish Plague.

CHAPTER 2

CATCHING CRAWFISH

My memories of fishing for crawfish date back to my young teens. I was growing up in California and I loved to fish. There wasn't a weekend, day off of school or vacation that I wasn't fishing. It was on a quick summer vacation along the Southern California coast when I caught Crawfish Fever. We were camped near the beach and due to a wild undertow current I found myself confined to the campground.

At the north end of the campground, a small creek entered into a freshwater lagoon before entering into the sea. I remember standing underneath a wooden railroad bridge that had a distinct smell of tar. When the ocean breeze funneled through the wood pilings the smell of tar mixed with the sweet smell of the ocean and left a memorable imprint on my brain. As I looked into the shallow murky water, I could see the ground move. The shallow ledge of water plants and small rocks was covered with crawfish. LOBSTER, I yelled as I raced back to camp! I soon learned that they were not lobsters but a near cousin - the crawfish.

I spent the next two days catching hundreds of these delicious little crustaceans and I have been hooked on crawfish ever since. Now that I am in my late forties and living hundreds of miles away from that original secret crawfish hole, I still take every opportunity possible to catch these little critters.

I introduced my children to crawfish at a young age. Some of my best outdoor memories are of my children with a string attached to a chicken leg covered with crawfish. The smiles on their faces were priceless.

Catching crawfish is fun for the whole family and your friends. It is a great opportunity to get together as a group and enjoy the outdoors. The feast that follows is also memorable!

Crawfish Techniques and Gear

Determining best location- Crawfish like cover and ample food sources. Most of a crawfish diet is going to be small aquatic life and plants. The best location is going to be in areas that have both cover and food. Areas with submerged rocks and crevices work well. Also, areas of thick underwater vegetation produce good numbers of crawfish. Most of the crawfish that you catch will be in water from 1 foot to 10 feet in depth.

Rocky Shorelines give crawfish protection

Rocks and underwater vegetation means crawfish

Bait

What is the best bait to use for catching crawfish? This depends on the time of year and the temperature of the water. It also depends on the preferences of the person fishing.

In cooler water I like to use fish or chicken as bait. It is very important that you check your state fishing regulations before using any fish as bait. In most states, it is illegal to use any parts of a game fish for bait to catch crawfish.

As soon as the water warms up, I fish a little deeper and with manufactured baits, chicken, turkey or any other meat.

Crawfish bait must be fresh! I use to think that crawfish bait had to be extra stinky to attract the little crustaceans. However, contrary to my belief, crawfish don't like spoiled, smelly or aged bait.

I found that out the hard way recently while fishing at Strawberry reservoir. I had several chicken legs that I left out to spoil. When they were sufficiently smelly, I tied them to my string and put some in my trap. I thought for sure that the crawfish would go wild for this smelly bait. To my great surprise, I caught very few crawfish.

Hand Line – this is probably the most common way that people catch crawfish, especially if they are with small children or not catching them for commercial purposes. A hand line is just that – a line. Any twine will work. I recommend that you cut a piece of twine about 25 feet long. This will allow you to fish at different depths.

Bait on the end of the hand line

When fishing with a hand line, tie your bait to the end of the line with a slip knot.

Once the bait is secured to the line begin fishing. Start close in and work out until you find the greatest concentration of crawfish. In many cases the crawfish will just move to where your bait is located. However, there has been many times when fishing that the crawfish seem to be concentrated in certain areas.

Once you locate crawfish, make sure your hand line is baited with fresh bait. Let your bait sit for 3-5 minutes or longer if necessary. Once the bait is covered with crawfish pull in.

Very important – it is necessary to pull the hand line in slowly. A quick movement of the bait will scare the crawfish off your bait and into their protective layer. Also, try to keep your shadow off of the water and crawfish. Shadows and excessive movement in the water will scare many crawfish off the bait.

As you pull the hand line closer to you, take your net and gently submerge it behind the bait and crawfish. Once the net is in position, gently lift the bait off the bottom and position the net under the bait and crawfish. Scoop upwards and out of the water. If you have completed these steps your net will be filled with tasty crawfish.

Net full of crawfish

Net – If you are going to be using a hand line from shore to catch crawfish, then it is very important that you have a small mesh net to scoop the crawfish out of the water. Don't try to lift the crawfish out of the water and then over to your bucket or cooler. They will fall off and you will lose them. If you do not have a net, a plastic or metal strainer will work well.

Traps

There are many types of crawfish traps on the market. Every manufacture of traps will claim that their trap catches more crawfish then their competitors. I will leave that argument up to you to decide. Any of the traps pictured below will work just fine to catch crawfish.

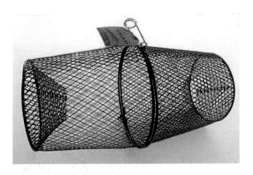

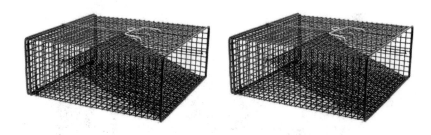

Placement of your Traps

The traps should be placed in areas that provide cover for the crawfish such as rocks, roots, or other structure. These areas provide cover for the crawfish but the algae which grows In these areas is also a food base for the crawfish. Crawfish will be concentrated in areas of good structure because they will use this to their advantage. In Utah where I catch crawfish, the lakes are full of Cutthroat and Rainbow Trout that are always on the lookout for a shellfish meal.

Many lakes have depth and structure charts that are used by boaters and fishermen alike. If you have access to these charts, use them to locate areas where crawfish would be concentrated. The best areas have a lot of rocks. Areas where rocks shore up a dam or bank of a river are excellent locations for placement of traps. Areas of heavy underwater vegetation are also excellent locations to set your traps.

The best bait for crawfish traps would be chicken, turkey, dog food, or manufactured crawfish bait. Manufactured baits are mostly used in the commercial crawfish industry but can be bought by individuals on the internet.

Make sure that your traps are located in 5 to 15 feet of water. These depths are the best for traps. If you have access to a boat, you can set multiple traps around the body of water that you are fishing. Just like in crab or lobster fishing, you will need to mark your traps so you can find them when it is time to pull them. An inexpensive way to mark your traps is to tie an old plastic detergent or milk container to the end of the Line. You can paint these containers a bright fluorescent orange if you want to be able to see them easier at night.

Best time to catch crawfish

The best time to catch crawfish is in the evening and during the nighttime hours. Crawfish are predators that come out at night to catch their prey. Nighttime also gives the crawfish protection from other predators that are looking for a quick meal. Fishing with traps works especially well at night. Set your traps in the early evening and let them sit for a few hours or overnight. If you are going to let them soak overnight, make sure that there is plenty of bait in your traps. Crawfish are ravenous feeders and if you don't have enough bait they will clean the trap out and move on.

Fishing during the day is also productive with hand lines. Focus on areas with heavy coverage or rock piles. Fishing in these protected areas works best during daylight hours. The crawfish will be hiding out to avoid predators but are opportunistic feeders and will latch on to your bait.

Crawfish Outings are Fun!

One thing is certain, if you go fishing for crawfish you will have a great time. Young or old, you will have a smile on your face as you catch these little lobsters. Crawfish outings are a group affair and should be enjoyed by family and friends. There is nothing better than a day on the lake with your family and friends enjoying the outdoors and catching your own dinner.

After a day on the lake, it is time for a crawfish boil. Summer evenings spent over a long table piled high with red delicious crawfish caught earlier that day is a feast meant for a king.

If you want to make memories that will last forever, take up the sport of crawfish fishing. **Be careful, fishing for crawfish is habit forming!**

CHAPTER 3

HANDLING, CLEANING AND COOKING CRAWFISH

Handling Crawfish at the Lake or River

Crawfish are delicious if you handle them and prepare them properly. The most important aspect of good tasting crawfish is what you do with them as soon as they come out of the water. Many people put them in a bucket of water on the bank in direct sun. This is not the best way to store your catch, unless you are very diligent. There are two issues with storing crawfish this way. 1. The water will heat up quickly and kill the crawfish. 2. If the heat does not kill them, then the lack of oxygen will, especially if you have a significant amount of crawfish in the bucket. If you are going to use a bucket, make sure that you keep the water cool and constantly refresh the bucket with new oxygenated water.

The best way to store crawfish would be in cool place, like an ice chest, with some ice on the crawfish to keep them cool. Crawfish will live in the ice chest for an extended period of time as long as the temperature does not reach below 32 degrees. If you store crawfish in an ice chest with ice they will appear to be lethargic or even dead. However, once they warm up, they will come back to life.

Cleaning Crawfish

Once you are home or at the location where you will have the crawfish boil, it is time to clean the crawfish. You will need plenty of fresh water and more ice.

If you are at home, the kitchen sink will work well when cleaning the crawfish. Place them in the sink and discard any dead crawfish, plant debris, rocks and dirt. Once you have these items removed from the crawfish, rinse them vigorously to clean off the shells and underbodies of the crawfish. I use a set of tongs to gently move the crawfish around as I rinse them off. It is very important for both taste and esthetics that you clean the crawfish as best as possible.

Some people like to purge the crawfish before they boil them. Purging crawfish is the processes of having the crawfish excrete all of their intestinal debris. There is no quick way to do this. The best way to purge a crawfish is to keep them alive for several days and do not feed them. However, this method can be time consuming and labor intensive.

Some people swear that if you put them in salt water they will purge themselves very quickly. My experience has been that the salt water method does not work and kills the crawfish before they purge.

I would recommend that you not try to purge the crawfish. It is easier to just remove the intestine (the vain) after cooking and before you eat the crawfish. I will explain how to remove the vain in the next section.

Once the crawfish are rinsed and thoroughly cleaned, it is time to put them in the boiling pot of water. If you are not going to immediately cook the crawfish you will need to store them in a cool location on ice.

Boiling Crawfish

Now it is time to cook the crawfish. There are many different ways to prepare crawfish. The recipe in this book is just one way to cook crawfish. The internet is full of different types of recipes for cooking these little lobsters.

Almost all of the preparations start out with boiling or steaming the crawfish. Crawfish can be boiled in plain water but most recipes call for a seasoned water boil that consists of different spices, corn and potatoes.

Crawfish need to boil for at least 10-15 minutes depending on the number of crawfish in the pot. Once they all turn red and have had sufficient amount of time to cook they are drained and eaten.

Boiled crawfish

How to Eat Crawfish

There are many ways to tackle eating a crawfish. I am going to list the 6 steps I use to eat a crawfish. I recommend you do the following.

1. **Separate the head from the tail.** You can accomplish this by holding the tail in one hand while the other hand twists the head. The twisting motion will separate the crawfish easily and you will end up with half the crawfish in each hand.

2. **Suck the Body.** If you are not squeamish about sucking the bodies of the crawfish then proceed to suck the juices out of the head and body. Some people also like to pull the top shell of the body and eat the green "butter" in the body. This is a delicacy in many parts of the world.

3. **Crack the tail shell.** To access the delicate and most substantial portion of meat, pinch the tail between two fingers and crack the shell. You can now either access the tail meat or proceed to just remove the entire shell from the tail.

4. **Devein the tail meat.** Once you have removed the tail meat it is important to take the vein out of the tail. Hold the tail meat with one hand and peel back the outer skin. The vein will be pulled off with the outer layer of skin. Discard this vein.

   Before you shell the tail, you can also devein the tail by twisting the middle flipper gently to the right or left while pulling the flipper out. The flipper will come of with the vein attached. It is important to devein the crawfish in order to avoid a muddy tasting piece of meat.

5. **Eat the tail meat.** Once the meat is shelled and deveined eat the tail meat.

6. **Suck or eat the claws.** Crack open the claws and if the meat is substantial enough to eat, remove and eat. If the claws are too small to eat, suck the juices out of the claw.

Cooking Crawfish

I love to eat crawfish. I also love that there are many different ways to prepare these delicious little fresh water crustaceans. If you are interested in trying a great recipe for a spicy, garlicky, buttery and delicious crawfish I recommend that you try the recipes that follow.

As I mentioned there are lots of different recipes. There are Gumbos, Etouffes, bisques, stocks pasta sauces, sandwiches and breads. Go on the internet and look up these many different recipes. To your surprise, you will find that there is more to eating crawfish than in the traditional boil!

Nutritional Information - Crawfish are an excellent source of protein. Crawfish tail meat is very lean with only about 1% of your daily allowance of fat. Crawfish are low in calories, fat and saturated fat, and are a good source of vitamins.
Vitamins found in crawfish –

- Calcium
- Niacin
- VitaminB-6
- Vitamin B-12
- Protein
- Biotin
- Iron
- Phosphorus
- Selenium
- Vitamin A

It will take about 7 pounds of live crawfish to yield one pound of tail meat. Make sure that you eat more than just the tail meat. Sucking the meat and juices out of the head is also a great treat!

Nutrition Facts	
Crayfish, cooked	
Amount Per 3 oz (85 g)	
Calories 74	
% Daily Value*	
Total Fat 1.1 g	1%
Saturated fat 0.2 g	1%
Polyunsaturated fat 0.4 g	
Monounsaturated fat 0.2 g	
Cholesterol 116 mg	38%
Sodium 82 mg	3%
Potassium 202 mg	5%
Total Carbohydrate 0 g	0%
Dietary fiber 0 g	0%
Protein 15 g	30%
Vitamin A	0%
Calcium	4%
Vitamin B-6	5%
Magnesium	7%
*Percent Daily Values are based on a 2,000 calorie diet.	

CHAPTER 4

GREAT CRAWFISH RECIPES

Asian Cajun Crawfish Boil – this is my favorite way to prepare crawfish. It is spicy, garlicky, buttery and delicious!

Ingredients

Shellfish

1-2 pound crawfish or shellfish per person

Boil

1 package crab boil

1 lemon – quartered

Garlic Sauce

3 heads of garlic, chopped (fresh is best)

2 cups of margarine (4 sticks)

1 tablespoon of Old Bay Seasoning

1 tablespoon of Cayenne Pepper

1 tablespoon of Paprika

1 tablespoon Lemon Pepper

1 tablespoon dry chicken bullion

Tony's Magic Dust

1 tablespoon Old Bay Seasoning

1 tablespoon Paprika

1 tablespoon Garlic Powder

1 tablespoon dry chicken bouillon

1 tablespoon Cayenne Pepper (optional)

INSTRUCTIONS

1. Poor live crawfish or shellfish into sink and wash until water runs clear and all dirt and grime is washed away. Discard dead crawfish/shellfish
2. Cook shell fish in boiling water with crab boil package and 1 quartered lemon.
3. Make the sauce; melt the 2 cups of margarine in a saucepan.
4. Add 3 heads of chopped garlic to melted butter. Cook garlic until translucent.
5. Once the garlic is translucent, add ;
   a. 1 tbsp Old Bay Seasoning
   b. 1 tbsp Paprika
   c. 1 tbsp lemon pepper

    d. 1 tbsp dry chicken bouillon

    e. 1 tbsp cayenne pepper (add more for extra heat)

6. Simmer the sauce for 10 minutes and check for flavor. Add more seasoning as desired.

7. Put shell fish in a large plastic cooking bag or bowel, pour sauce over shell fish and toss with the sauce.

8. Sprinkle Tony's Magic Dust over the crawfish as desired before serving.

Louisiana Crawfish Boil

Makes: 10 to 15 servings

1 (35-pound) live crawfish

1 (12-ounce) bottle Crystal Hot Sauce

1 to 2 (26-ounce) boxes of table salt

3 ounces Zatarain's Shrimp & Crab Boil liquid concentrate (3/4 of a 4-ounce bottle)

3 ounces cayenne pepper

8 to 10 medium new potatoes, such as Red Bliss or Yukon gold

4 small yellow onions cut in half

INSTRUCTIONS

1. Find out if your crawfish have been purged. If they haven't, soak in fresh water for 10 minutes.

2. While you're waiting, fill an 80-quart pot halfway with water and bring to a boil over a large outdoor burner over high heat. Add hot sauce, salt, Zatarain's, and cayenne pepper.

3. Add potatoes and onions to the pot. Boil vegetables for about 10 minutes.

4. Add half the crawfish to the pot. After 5 minutes turn off the heat, cover, and let the crawfish steep to absorb the flavors for 15 to 20 minutes. Drain and dump onto the table. Repeat with the rest of the crawfish (you can boil 2 to 3 batches of crawfish in the same water-seasoning mixture).
5. Eat plain or with dipping' sauces like cocktail sauce, mayonnaise, ketchup, or Tabasco.

Crawfish Bread
Serves 4–5

INGREDIENTS:
2 cups peeled crawfish tails
1 loaf French bread
1/2 stick butter
1/2 cup diced onions
1/2 cup diced celery
1/4 cup diced red bell peppers
1 tbsp minced garlic

1/2 tsp dry mustard
1/2 cup mayonnaise
1/3 cup Mozzarella cheese
1/3 cup Cheddar cheese

INSTRUCTIONS
Slice French bread in half lengthwise and scoop out the inside of the loaf. Set aside. In a large skillet, melt butter over medium-high heat. Sauté crawfish, onions, celery, bell peppers and garlic for 15 minutes. Blend in dry mustard and mayonnaise. Add cheeses and blend until melted. Spread crawfish mixture inside the bread then put halves back together. Butter the top of the loaf, wrap it in foil and bake on a barbecue pit or in a 350°F oven for 20–30 minutes. Cut bread into slices and serve hot.

Creamy Crawfish Pasta
Serves 6-8

1/2 cup (1 stick) unsalted butter
1 green bell pepper, diced small
1 onion, diced small
2 stalks celery, diced small

3 cloves garlic, minced
1/4 cup all-purpose flour
1 heaping teaspoon tomato paste
1/2 cup dry white wine
1 pound frozen cooked crawfish tails, thawed
1 cup half and half or heavy cream
1 teaspoon Creole seasoning
Red pepper flakes, to taste
Kosher salt and freshly ground pepper, to taste
16 ounces penne pasta, cooked according to package directions
Chopped parsley, for serving

INSTRUCTIONS

In a large Dutch oven, melt butter over medium heat. Add the bell peppers, onions, and celery, and sauté until tender, about 7-8 minutes. Add the garlic and cook for an additional minute. Stir in the flour until the vegetables are well-coated and no white clumps remain. Stir in the tomato paste until completely combined.

Increase the heat to medium-high. Add the wine and crawfish to the Dutch oven; let the wine simmer out for a couple of minutes. Pour in the heavy cream. Add the Creole seasoning, a generous pinch of red pepper flakes, 1 teaspoon salt, and freshly ground pepper. Cook the sauce at a gentle boil until it is thickened and coats the back of the spoon, about 5 - 10 minutes. Adjust seasoning to taste.

Fold the cooked penne into the crawfish sauce. Stir in a handful of chopped parsley. Serve the crawfish pasta with additional red pepper flakes, hot sauce, freshly grated Parmesan, and slices of toasted garlic bread.

Crawfish Etouffee

Serves 6-8

INGREDIENTS

1/2 cup butter, cubed

1/2 cup plus 2 tablespoons all-purpose flour

1-1/4 cups chopped celery

1 cup chopped green pepper

1/2 cup chopped green onions

1 can (14-1/2 ounces) chicken broth1 cup water

1/4 cup minced fresh parsley

1 tablespoon tomato paste

1 bay leaf

1/2 teaspoon salt

1/4 teaspoon pepper

1/4 teaspoon cayenne pepper

2 pounds cooked crawfish tail meat.

Hot cooked rice

INSTRUCTIONS

1. In a large heavy skillet, melt butter; stir in flour. Cook and stir over low heat for about 20 minutes until mixture is a caramel-colored paste. Add the celery, pepper and onions; stir until coated. Add the broth, water, parsley, tomato paste, bay leaf, salt, pepper and cayenne pepper. Bring to a boil.

2. Reduce heat; cover and simmer for 30 minutes, stirring occasionally. Discard bay leaf. Add crawfish and heat through. Serve over rice.

Crawfish Bisque

5 lbs. boiled crawfish

1/2 medium onion, cut up

2 cloves garlic, crushed

1 rib celery, cut up and chopped

1/2 red bell pepper, chopped

1/2 cup dry white wine

1/2 cup brandy

1 small lemon, sliced

2/3 cup flour

5 sprigs Italian parsley leaves, chopped

2 green onions, sliced finely

Salt

Tabasco

INSTRUCTIONS

1. Rinse the boiled crawfish with lukewarm water to remove some of the salt, which will otherwise get concentrated later.

Peel all of the crawfish and reserve the tail meat and the shells separately. Get some kid to pull off all the claws from the shells. Put all the claws into a heavy plastic bag. Using a meat mallet, bash the claws enough to break most of them.

2. In an eight-quart (or larger) saucepan, sauté the onions, garlic, celery, and bell pepper over medium heat until the vegetables are browned at the edges.

3. Add the crawfish claws, shells and wine, and bring to a boil. When most of the liquid has evaporated, pour the brandy over the shells. If you are comfortable with flaming dishes and have a fire extinguisher nearby, carefully touch a flame to the brandy. Let the flames die out. Otherwise, just let the brandy boil away.

4. Add the lemon and enough water to cover all the shells. Bring it to a boil, and then lower to the lowest possible simmer. Simmer for

thirty minutes, spooning out the scum from the top of the pot every now and then.

5. Strain the stock into another saucepan and discard the solids. Simmer until reduced to about three quarts. Strain through a fine sieve. (At this point, the stock can be refrigerated for up to three days or frozen for later use.)

6. In a large saucepan over medium-low heat, make a dark roux with the flour and butter, stirring constantly to avoid burning. When the roux is the color of chocolate, stir it into the crawfish stock with a wire whisk until completely blended.

7. Add parsley and green onions. Reserve six large crawfish tails per person. In a food processor, chop the rest of the crawfish tail meat to a near-puree. Add this to the soup and return to a simmer for five minutes. Add salt and hot sauce to taste.

6. Place the whole crawfish tails in soup plates, and ladle the bisque over them.

Sichuan Crawfish

INGREDIENTS:

2 lbs crawfish
10 cloves garlic (peel the skin and lightly pounded)
5 sprigs cilantro
5 slices fresh ginger
2 tablespoon soy sauce
10-15 dried red chillies (depends how spicy you want)
1 tablespoon **Sichuan peppercorns**
2 tablespoons cooking oil
1 teaspoon chicken boullion powder
1 tablespoon sugar
1/2 teaspoon sesame oil
1/2 cup water
Salt to taste

Rinse them a few times with cold running water until they are
thoroughly clean. Heat up a pan or wok with the cooking oil. Add in
garlic cloves, ginger, dried chillies, Sichuan peppercorns until spicy
and aromatic. Toss in the crawfish and stir continuously for 1-2
minutes. Add in all the seasonings, water, and cilantro and cover
the wok for 5 minutes. Dish out and serve hot.

Crawfish Salad Rolls (Mini Lobster Roll)

INGREDIENTS

1 pound cooked crawfish tails finely chopped
1/2 cup mayonnaise
Fresh lemon juice, to taste
Fresh chives, chopped
Old Bay Seasoning or Cajun seasoning, to taste
12 small soft dinner rolls (or quality hot dog buns)
Melted, clarified butter (for brushing on bread)

INSTRUCTIONS

Combine lobster, mayonnaise, lemon juice, chives and seasoning in a small bowl.

Cut rolls or buns quartered crosswise. Brush cut sides with butter. Working in batches, toast cut sides of rolls or buns until golden brown. Fill each roll or bun with a little crawfish salad. Garnish with extra chive.

Swedish Crawfish Recipe

INGREDIENTS

6 pounds (2.5kg) live crayfish or Louisiana crawfish
2/3 cup coarse sea salt
3 tablespoons sugar
3 bottles dark beer, preferably an English stout
1 large bunch fresh dill, plus a few sprigs for garnish
Lemon wedges
Mayonnaise and thin slices good white bread (optional)

PREPARATION:

-

Put the crayfish in the sink under cold running water to make sure they are alive. Discard any that do not move.

-

In a large pot, combine 2 gallons cold water, the salt, sugar, beer, and dill and bring to a boil over high heat. Add the crayfish, return to a boil, and turn off the heat. Let stand for an hour or two before serving.

-

Drain the crayfish and arrange on a large serving platter. Garnish with dill and squeeze some lemon juice over them.

-

Crack open the shells at the table and carefully remove the crayfish meat. Place the meat on white bread spread with mayonnaise, or eat it just as it is, with a drop of lemon juice. The white meat in the tail is the best, but the meat from the head is also delicious; do not eat the papery gills.

Italian Crawfish Diavolo (Spicy Sauce)

INGREDIENTS
½ cup extra-virgin olive oil
2 (1¼-lb.) cleaned and cooked crawfish tails and about a dozen
cooked whole crawfish
½ cup flour
2 tsp. crushed red chile flakes
1 tsp. dried oregano
5 cloves garlic, finely chopped
2 tbsp. tomato paste
½ cup cognac or brandy
1 cup seafood or fish stock
1 (28-oz.) can whole peeled tomatoes in juice, crushed
1 bay leaf
Kosher salt and freshly ground black pepper, to taste
1 lb. bucatini pasta, cooked
1 tbsp. chopped parsley

INSTRUCTIONS

Heat oil in an 8-qt. Dutch oven over medium-high heat. Toss crawfish (including whole cooked crawfish)) in flour, shake off excess, and add to pot; cook about 6 minutes. Transfer crawfish to a plate; set aside. Add chile flakes, oregano, and garlic to pot; cook until lightly toasted, about 3 minutes. Add tomato paste; cook until lightly caramelized, about 2 minutes. Add cognac; cook until almost evaporated, about 2 minutes. Add stock, tomatoes, and bay leaf; boil. Reduce heat to medium-low; cook, partially covered, until thickened, about 30 minutes. Add crawfish to sauce and heat for about 5 minutes or until hot. Season with salt and pepper. Add pasta; toss with sauce. Transfer to a large serving platter; sprinkle with parsley.